PROVIDING HELP FOR THE COMMUNITY AND NEIGHBORHOODS

CHARISMATA

HOMES MAGAZINE

Charismata
Homes & Company

www.charismatahomesandcompany.com

Printed by CreateSpace, An Amazon.com Company

PROVIDING HELP FOR THE COMMUNITY AND NEIGHBORHOODS

CHARISMATA

HOMES MAGAZINE

EDITOR-IN-CHIEF
Michelle Henry
charismata630@gmail.com

GRAPHIC/WEB DESIGNER
D. Bailey
dbailey@indiefaith.com

ADVERTISEMENT MANAGER
Michelle Henry
advertise@charismatahomesandcompany.com

PHOTOGRAPHERS
My Touch Productions
Dee Head
D. Bailey

CONTRIBUTORS
Sisters In Spirit Book Club

COPY ORDERS & ADVERTISING OFFICE
Send Money Order or Check to:
Charismata Homes
18642 W. McNichols
Detroit, Michigan 48219
(248) 773-2866

Copy Order Item #:
Charismata Magazine Issue #3 2016
S&H Plus Retail Price - $9.99 per copy

WWW.CHARISMATAHOMESANDCOMPANY.COM
Printed by CreateSpace, An Amazon.com Company

Charismata
Homes & Company

Magazine cover: PROVIDING HELP FOR THE COMMUNITY AND NEIGHBORHOODS — CHARISMATA HOMES MAGAZINE, featuring MUSIC FASHION ENTERTAINMENT. ANNUAL PROGRAMS GIVES HOPE — CHARISMATA HOMES OFFERING PROGRAMS TO FAMILIES IN NEED. PLUS MORE. LOCAL HAIR AND NAIL STYLIST IS BRINGING 2014 A WHOLE NEW LOOK TO MICHIGAN. Michelle Dixson — HELPING THE COMMUNITY WITH LOVE AND DEDICATION. Tez Rippa — ALL NEW RAP ARITIST TEZ RIPPA HEATS UP THE MIDWEST WITH A WHOLE NEW SOUND. APRIL 2014 No.1 WWW.CHARISMATAHOMES.COM

CONTENTS

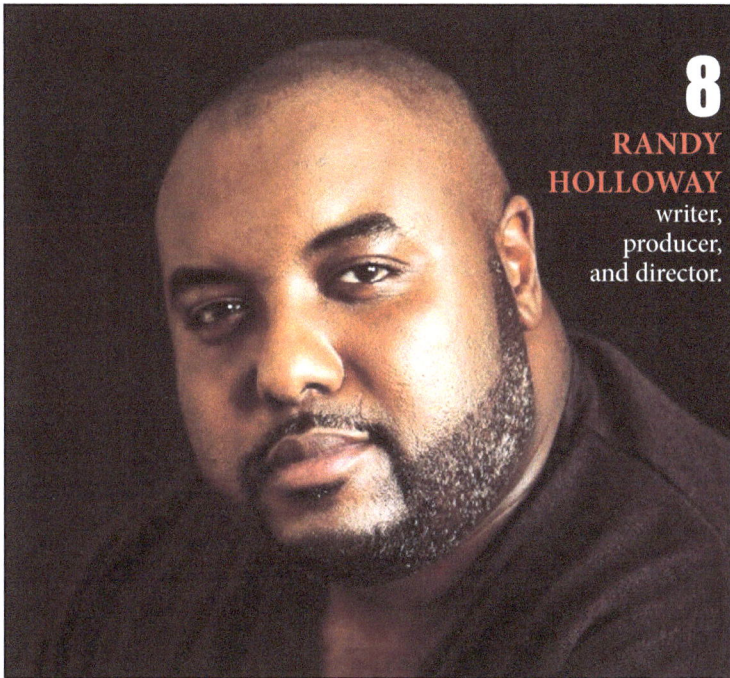

8
RANDY HOLLOWAY
writer, producer, and director.

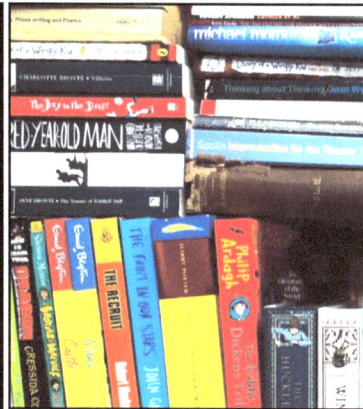

16
SISTER'S IN SPIRIT BOOK CLUB
talks about their program.

20
THOMAS VALENTINE
On a journey of life while finding time to author a new book and more.

26
MARIAH DIXSON
Featuring hair and nails in the exclusive styles.

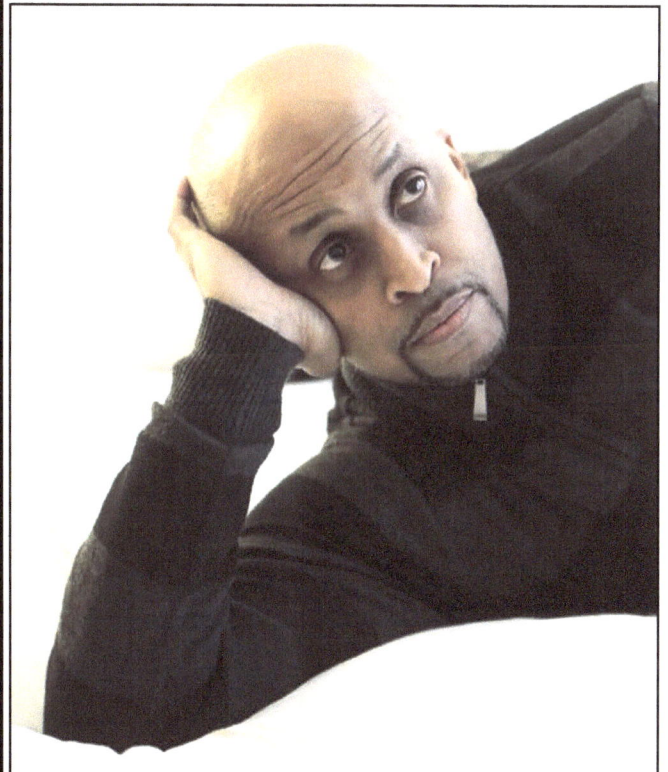

Hope for Detroit Internet Talk Show

EDDIE P IS SHOWCASING PEOPLE DOING POSITIVE THINGS IN THE METRO DETROIT COMMUNITY.

by Michelle Henry

The photo is Eddie P host of Hope For Detroit Internet Talk Show on the set. This show showcasing people doing positive things in the Metro-Detroit community by interviewing them in businesses, entrepreneurs and in the entertaiment segways. The staff also, includes Keith Robinson, Producer, Gail Roberts, Co-Producer, various associated staff members.

The shows are taped and downloaded on a weblink called Vimeo so the show can be sent and played anytime. We taped our shows on Saturdays at 1:00 pm at Detroit Trade Market at 8500 E. 8 Mile Rd 2 blocks E of Van Dyke in the Belliere Shopping.

Email: talkofthetown23@gmail.com
Phone: (313) 330-9094

MAJIK TOUCH DANCE COMPANY

19200 Livernois Detroit, MI 48221   PH: (313) 778-1209   www.majiktouchdance.com

Kim Frager - Co Owner, Head Choreographer and the dynamic creative force of Majik Touch Dance Company. Before opening her own studio she had over 20 years of competitive teaching experience in cheerleading and dance. Coach Kim holds the record of longest winning 1st place coach in the history of the Detroit Police Athletic League (PAL). Because of this and other numerous awards and achievements many want to be under the teaching of Coach Kim. She directly manages all aspects of the studio's operations, including team creations and development, choreography designs, coach development, and is the final say on all of our dance teams. Since opening MTDC Kim continues to do what she does best and that is "WIN". Majik Touch is a competitive Hip-Hop dance team that travels from state to state. The dance teams range from ages 5-18 years, both male and female dancers.   Our Hip-Hop Dance Teams are National, Grand National, and US Final Champions. First in the country to be ranked TOP DAWG on all age levels. Majik Touch also ranks as one of the best top three teams in the nation in competitive hip-hop dance. One of the many goals that Coach Kim has set for Majik Touch is to support and reinforce programs that promote community pride. Located on the Avenue of Fashion MTDC has been involved with numerous events to help in the revival of the Avenue. Asking Coach Kim why dance she speaks loudly "Dance is simply the language used to keep idle minds active, enhance academic and social performance and communicate life lessons while creating a healthy and successful lifestyle. Coach Kim along with her husband Coach Darryl Frager has impacted the lives of so many of our youth and their names continue to be a cornerstone in our community.

BEAUTIFUL LITTLE BUTTERFLIES

Transformation

After School Program for Girls

First session----September 12, 2016 thru December 16, 2016

Beautiful Little Butterflies After School Program operates in conjunction with the Wayne County School Calendar. The program begins on Monday, September 14th. We provide countless activities based on the components of wellness: physical, emotional, spiritual, environmental, intellectual and social. This curriculum, with an emphasis on completing homework, allows Beautiful Little Butterflies after school program provide a well-rounded experience for the girls. Girls will participate in arts and crafts and field trips, interacting with special guests and positive role models, and much more. We are also offering a Robotics Program in which girls will learn engineering skills to help close the academic gap in math and science among boys and girls.

REASONABLE RATES:

Monday-----Friday

3;30 pm-6:30pm

Ages: 7yrs-12yrs old   Ages 13yrs-15yrs old

Every other Saturday 12-noon-2pm Etiquette Classes $15.00

$10 Registration fee non refundable per child

Registration $25.00 non refundable per child

$50.00 per week - $200.00 monthly

Requirements: Purchases of T-Shirt $ 25.00   Copy of shot records-Birth certificate-Physical

Requirements: Purchases of T-Shirt $ 25.00
Copy of shot records-Birth certificate-Physical

Charismata

18642 W McNichols
Detroit, MI. 48219
Phone: 248-773-2866

A Real Community Superwoman

MICHELLE HENRY GIVES BACK TO HER COMMUNITY WHERE SHE WAS BORN AND RAISED. ALSO HELPING HOMELESS WOMEN AND CHILDREN.

by Michelle Henry

In 2006, my family and I moved from a small home in Detroit, Michigan to Southfield Michigan. My dream was to help make a positive impact on children in the foster care system; babies, older children and sibling groups who were often overlooked by society. I was raised around families that had adopted children in their family from the foster care system, so knew the struggle that came with not having family support.

Later, my husband and I adopted sibyls of two sisters in need. Since the goal always was to foster and then adopt an older sibling group, this fits nicely into our plans. Although my house wasn't ready for two more kids, we found a way to make it work. The new home in Southfield was a much bigger house; actually, it wasn't hard to accommodate the space. The story doesn't stop there, I had a new initiative, but to do so, they would need more bedrooms. We began buying hud houses and fixing them up while turning homes into transition homes for the sole purpose of helping others in need.

In 2009, as an addition to adoption, Michelle found the need to help homeless mothers with children. This idea was from a referral that a mother and her children were homeless. This wasn't an easy task considering I paid out of pocket to keep the homes up and running efficiently. I had no state funding and managed to keep houses open for families. Needless to say, I lost a two family flat to a tax auction which I use now as a learning tool.

In April 2013, I launched a new magazine "Charismata Homes Magazine" I had to find other ways to be creative and make extra money to help build food pantries, diaper pantries, personal items pantries, education material, clothes closet, and the upkeep of transitional housing. I have to say, I'm truly blessed to help people and each day there's a new mission.

If you're interested in donating to our organization, please visit our website: charismatahomesandcompany.com. Your donation will be a blessing.

Michelle Henry

Donation drop off:
Charismata Homes
18642 W Mcnichols
Detroit, MI 48219
Phone: (248) 773-2866

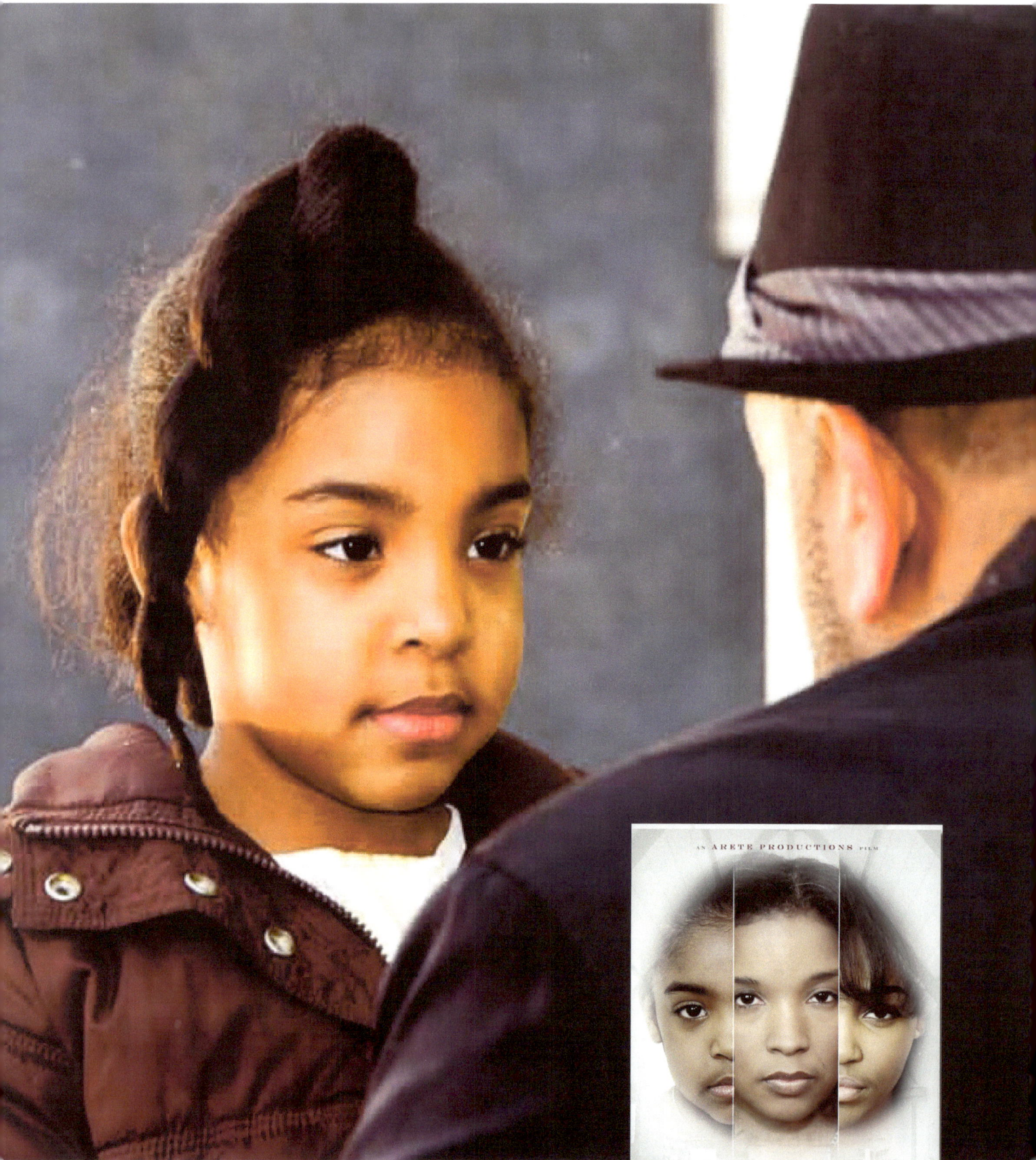

Award-Winning Producer

BORN IN DETROIT MICHIGAN, RANDY HOLLOWAY SOLD HIS FIRST TELEVISON SHOW TO A NATIONAL NETWORK.

by Michelle Henry

Award-winning writer, producer, and director Randy Holloway has been in the entertainment industry for nearly two decades having written, produced, and directed three feature-length films, including the groundbreaking film "Bianca Who Did This to You?" Randy has also produced a sitcom pilot, several reality shows, and has written numerous screenplays he currently has in development.

Mr. Holloway recently obtained a fellowship with the world-renowned Sundance Institute after submitting his coming of age screenplay titled "Making Money." Randy also has had the opportunity to learn about the nuances of the industry from some of the biggest names in entertainment including David Hill, Brad Pitt, Will Smith, Robert DeNiro, Paula Abdul, Jennifer Lopez, Christian Bale, and Sylvester Stallone to name a few.

Randy education and experience have allowed him to work with several major networks and studios including MTV, Oxygen Network, OWN, Columbia Pictures, and Fox to name a few. Randy was also part of the development team that recently sold the behind the scenes music show, "Vinyl Wars," to Punch TV network. Mr. Holloway is very grateful to have numerous committed people willing to sacrifice their own time and effort to support his own endeavors. His ultimate goal is to have his artistic contributions spawn and finance the careers of other budding talented professionals that he has had the pleasure of working with and mentoring.

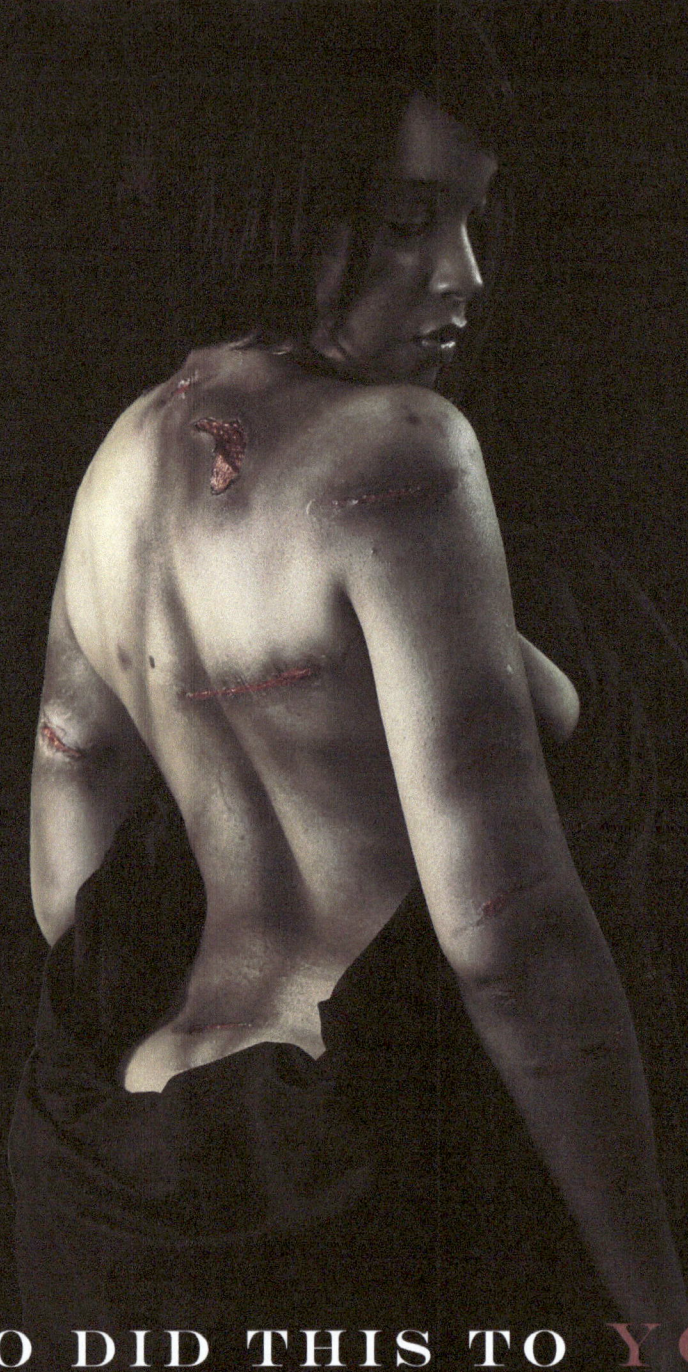

Local Actress in New Movie

BIANCA WHO DID THIS TO YOU?

by Michelle Henry

How did you get involved with the film Bianca? I got directly involved through a casting referral by "Bianca" director and long time friend, Randy Holloway. When I read the synopsis about the movie and ultimately the best selling Amazon book the movie is based off of ("Bianca Tell Us Who Did This to You"), it was very important to me that I auditioned for the role of "Bianca." Her story spoke to me and stirred something in me that I had to be involved in the project whether I landed the lead role or not.

What experiences allowed you to portray the character with such realism? I've never been physically abused or raped like "Bianca", however I do know what it's like to be taken advantage of to a certain degree. I'm a kind and trusting person that is always willing to lend a helping hand and especially when I was younger, it was to my disadvantage that I trusted the wrong people. Like many young women looking for love in all the wrong places, I've been involved with the wrong type of guy, who although they never laid a hand on me, were not very careful with my heart when it came to treating a young lady with the love and respect she deserves.

I've been on the receiving end of verbal and emotional abuse while in a relationship and there was a time in my life as a adolescent heading into young adulthood where I didn't value myself as I should have. I allowed myself to be treated unkind and went along with the flow, careful not to "rock the boat" when it came to demanding respect or saying "no" to behavior that was detrimental to my well-being. Underneath my warm, outgoing, confident exterior, I was angry, rebellious, careless at times and I didn't have a good sense of self-worth. I believe sub-consciously I tapped into all that to portray "Bianca."

From the time she was a child through her teenage years on into

adulthood, she suppressed a lot of pain, trauma and grief that resulted in displaced anger, self-destructive behavior and dysfunctional relationships with those she loved and or trusted. On an emotional level as a woman, I could relate to some of her pain from my own personal experiences. Before I was recast as "Bianca," I had proclaimed myself to be her. I wanted the role so bad. I just knew I was her. It wasn't until we went through the motions of rehearsing and preparing to film that I truly BECAME her.

What was your reaction to the responses you have been receiving about the film? The reaction I've received from starring in "Bianca" has been overwhelmingly positive. I've had people who I didn't know come up to me and commend me on my performance. Prior to "Bianca's" private press screening and theatrical premiere, Randy did some preliminary screen tests with different focus groups to gauge the audience reaction and I remember him sending me a private message on Facebook informing me that I had received rave reviews for my "authentic" performance as "Bianca."

The thing is there are thousands if not millions of "Biancas" around the world. Sadly, someone somewhere has been molested, raped, abused drugs, been assaulted, been beaten or violated in some way or they know someone that has and it spans across different ethnic groups, ages, backgrounds and social classes. Although it is more likely to happen to some than others, abuse knows no color, age, class or even gender. Anyone can be a "Bianca" and I think that is why this movie touches such a diverse group of people not to mention why people across the country are demanding to see "Bianca.

What was your most difficult scene to film during the production? I'd say for me initially I struggled with the scenes where I had to break down emotionally. I'm very sensitive to emotion so its usually not hard for me to show it. Sometimes I can't help it because I feel everything from my environment to the energy and emotions of others. You would think because I am empathetic and intuitive that it would come second nature to me but it didn't at first. The perfectionist in me always wants to put my best foot forward and nail it that I can tend to overthink sometimes of just doing or becoming. It was very important to me that I be believable in what I was portraying on screen. Ultimately, I had to let go of all that and just be in the moment.

What was the most difficult scene for you to watch during the screening?" It was difficult for me to watch myself totally break down on screen. I cried when I saw it. I couldn't believe how powerful it was. I was also proud though. I could feel my pain -- "Bianca's" pain jump off the screen and judging from the audience's reactions in the theater around me, everyone else could too. Outside of that, any scene in the movie involving the kids being molested or abused bothered me. One thing that always makes me mad is when someone mistreats or harms a child or an elderly person. They are so innocent and harmless that it really bothers me to see or hear about anyone that tries to take advantage of that for their own selfish gain or sick, twisted pleasure.

Talented Actress Qiana M

IS DETERMINED TO REACH A MILESTONE IN LIFE, AND HER GOAL IS TO BECOME A GLOBAL BRAND NAME WORLDWIDE.

by Michelle Henry

A woman of many talents and few passions, model/actress/writer/host Qiana M is determined to reach one ultimate goal becoming a global brand name. Her love affair with modeling began at the ripe age of ten and at the age of nineteen blossomed into a fully born pursuit, she's been smitten ever since booking gigs in fashion and commercial print, glamor, promotional modeling and music videos.

Since the fall of 2010, she has embarked on expanding her quest to become a global brand by entering the realm of acting. She has been blessed to have been cast as an extra in ABC's "Detroit 187", "Need for Speed", AMC's "Low Winter Sun", "Sparkle 2013" In addition to securing cameos in the background of major films. Ms. Davis can be found in supporting roles such as the groundbreaking Christian/Muslim romantic drama, "Aliah", antibullying short, "The Normals," controversial intra-racism stage play "Why Am I Black?" and the upcoming drama about sexual abuse and domestic violence, "Bianca Who Did This To You?"

Independent film company Commonality Productions believed in Qiana's star power as much that they cast her as the star and face of film short "Masquerade" as Ka-maya Sanchez, a single parent who turns to a life of a call girl to offset her child's mounting medical expenses after a tragic car accident. The buck doesn't stop there as this charming, multi-talented young woman is always putting herself in the position to obtain new opportunities in fashion/commercial print, runway, music video, film, and TV. Qiana M understands that it's not just through talent and hard work but a strong support system, faith in the almighty, a well-established network of resources and personal connections that get you to the top.

Rebuilding The Community

CHARISMATA PROVIDES MENTOR, EDUCATIONAL AND PARENTING WORKSHOPS FOR MOTHERS AND CHILDREN IN THE COMMUNITY.

by Michelle Henry

Charismata Homes is a nonprofit organization began five years ago, designed to help families in crisis. Charismata Homes was formed to specifically assist homeless mothers. Charismata is a valuable resource to help single mothers educate themselves about how manage as a single mother and navigate through daily living. We also assist them with their basic and more challenging needs.

Charismata provides mentor, educational, and parenting workshops. Clients are also granted furnished transitional housing.

Food Pantry: The food pantry is the **moms** hardship operation. The food pantry is one of the most progressive pantries in the area because of it's unique model. Guest to the pantry can visit every Tuesday, Thursday and Saturday with appointments only. Food is available to low income mothers and their children in the community. Food donations are needed to help build our pantry.

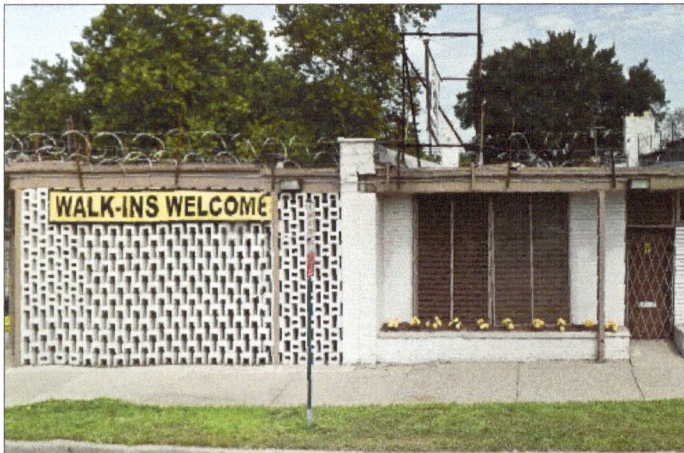

Personal Pantry: The personal pantry is available monthly on an emergency basis to assist mothers with the following personal items:

- Bar soap
- Laundry detergent
- Feminine hygiene products
- Toilet tissue
- Deodorant
- Shampoo
- Toothpaste

Emergency Baby Pantry: There is a constant need for items for emergency Baby Pantry such as diapers formula, baby wipes and newborn clothes. Other items include:

- Bottles
- Towels/washcloths
- Blankets
- Socks

Clothes Closet: Gently used clothing, shoes and linens are provided to our mothers and children. Donations are needed.
Career Clothes Closet: Is to provide a interview outfit an to help women gain the professional clothing that they need for a job.

Donation drop off:

Charismata Homes

18642 W Mcnichols

Detroit, MI 48219

Phone: (248) 773-2866

Charismata Homes & Company

Charismata Homes, a Detroit based Non - Profit Organization will hold their first Annual Charity Auction to bring awareness about Homeless Mothers with children in our community

Greater Giving Auction

Saturday - April 30, 2016
5:00PM until 9:30PM

Oakland Church of Christ
23333 W 10 Mi Rd Southfield , MI 48033

Guest Speaker
Formal Attire - Dinner included
Music - Entertainment - Raffle - Photographer
Donation: $50.00 per person
For more information please contact : 313 - 854 - 7537

Help bring awareness and support to Homeless Families
All Donations are Tax Debuctable
Early Bird Special : Purchase tickets by March 20th 2016
and recive $10.00 off each ticket

Purchase tickets online at : Charismatahomesandcompany.com
501 (c) (3) non - profit organization

Sisters in Spirit Book Club

SISTERS IN SPIRIT BOOK CLUB IS FORM OF 15 LADIES THAT COME TOGETHER MONTHLY TO DISCUSS BOOKS WITH TOPICS.

by Pam Evans

Sisters in Spirit Book Club is a group of 15 ladies that come together monthly to discuss books with relevant topics. The group was formed after eight friends attended a conference in Detroit featuring Maya Angelou! We were inspired to read so we held our first book club meeting in October of 1995. For 20 years we have been meeting every third Saturday. We read all genre of literature to enlighten and expand our minds and views of others and the world. Through the years we have hosted local authors, served at charitable events such as The Ronald McDonald House and given monetary gifts, food, clothing, etc. to worthy causes.

While we strive to reach out to help those in need, we also focus on edifying relationships with each other. Sisterly love is the key to maintaining long-term friendships. We also believe we are "blessed to be a blessing" and that is why we have partnered with Michele Henry and Charismata Homes. The work Mrs. Henry is doing is tremendous, and we are thankful we can play a small part in spreading love and hope to those who need a hand up. This is our third year partnering with Charismata Homes. We donated school supplies to the Back to School drive and have adopted four families for Christmas. The ladies are joyfully shopping for the children and mothers! We pray that Christmas for these families will be a little brighter because we care!

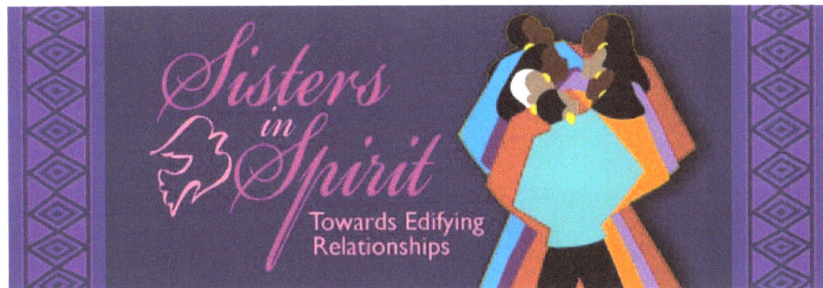

who supported Charismata Homes.

Ada Jones
WA.AJONES LLC

LaToya Scott
DMC Employee

Pamela Evans
Sisters in Spirit Book Club

Angie Young
Miracles for Moms & Babes

Stephanie Day, Jamie Reed, Allisha Brown "Lee's Cakes", Shantel Minor
Redford Church of Christ, Elaine Lloyd, Barbra Westley, Officer Lee, Kimberly Ross
Evelyn D. Scott, Sonora Swann, Rochester Hills Fire Department, Sylvia Whittington
Connie McCullough, Alana Turner and Sinai-Grance Pharmacy Department

CHARISMATA HOMES BOARD MEMBERS

Theodora Knight
Vice President

Yolonda Moye
Treasurer

Menoriva Ross
Volunteer Coach/Mentor

Constance McCullough
Volunteer/Mentor

JoVonna Williams
Secretary

David Greenway
Media Designer

Casino Bailey
Website Designer

FOR DONATIONS PLEASE VISIT: WWW.CHARISMATAHOMESANDCOMPANY.COM

The Gift of Warmth

GIVING THE GIFT OF WARMTH WITH HOMEMADE PILLOWS AND MORE TO CHARITY BY YOLANDA MOYE.

by Michelle Henry

Yolanda Moye

While so many of us love making things for family and friends. Yolanda Moye enjoys making hats and scarves for charities and service organizations in metro Detroit area. Yolanda reached out to Michelle Dixson-Henry at Charismata Homes and wanted to give back to the community and donated hats and scarves to Charismata Homes families. Yolanda plans to give back to other charities in the Detroit area during the winter.

Also, Yolanda will be donating hats and scarves during late fall and throughout the winter every year. Please support her goal by donating fabric to help achieve her purpose. Her passion is to help those in need, and she's presently working on a project opening a transitional home for mothers and children. In addition to Yolanda giving the gift of warmth pillows and giving back to the community with homeless families, she works full time at Henry Ford Hospital.

Independent Book Author

AUTHOR THOMAS VALENTINE RELEASES HIS NEW BOOK "UNINTENTIONALLY CONNECTED", ONLINE AND IN STORES NOW.

by Michelle Henry

His name is Thomas Valentine, also known as "Tommy." Tommy is a Detroit native and a graduate of Detroit Osborn high school. After graduation Tommy went on to Fort Valley State University in Fort Valley, Georgia and majored in journalism. Tommy loves sports but was unable to play do to a knee injury and turned his interest to the trumpet instead. He played the trumpet for a black college band and found a love for music greater than he could have ever imagined. After playing with the band for some time, Tommy joined the United States Navy, where he served from 1987 - 1991. His mission was with the Desert Shield, Desert Storm War and served as a Hospital Corpsman and Emergency Medical Rescue Recovery.

As a young teen, he aspired to become a teacher but was discouraged to do so from his peers. Tommy later discovered his love and passion for writing while in the Navy. He wrote stories, songs, and poems while he was in combat and knew that this was his calling. Now at 51, Tommy is achieving his dreams, writing stories, novels and hopefully movies one day. He recently published his first book "Unintentionally Connected" which is available online now at Amazon.com Tommy wants people to know you're never too old to follow a dream or passion and never let anyone ever talk you out of doing something positive that you love. Tommy is happily married to Mia Valentine, they have three children, and Tommy has two kids from a previous marriage.

If anyone has any questions or feedback about his book and would like his ghostwriting services send Tommy an email at valentinesdaymedia22@gmail.com. All feedback is welcome! Tommy says

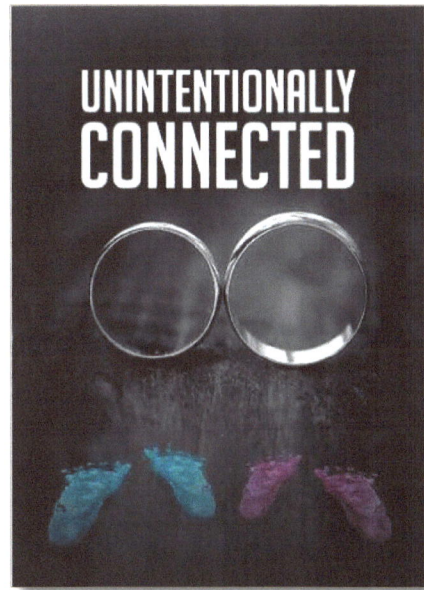

the positive gives him more confidence, and the negative gives him strength. Tommy new year's resolution this year is to complete four fictional novels and seek and sign to a movie deal. Keep me in your prayers and thanks for your support.

Meet Michelle Dixson

THIS SUPERWOMAN REALLY LOVES TO HELP WOMEN AND CHILDREN.
HER MISSION IS TO HELP THEM OFF THE STREET INTO SAFE HOUSING.

by Micheal Hall

I was a single mother raising four children. Motherhood taught me about patience, compassion and empathy. I learned how to enjoy the ride and not be the driver. My children learned how to be grateful for what they had and optimistic about what the future would hold them if they continued to go down the correct pathway. As a single mother, it wasn't easy surviving the storms. My children have witnessed poverty, hunger and unfulfilled needs. I came a long way providing and keeping my children safe. I raised my children in the church and always kept the faith that God would send me a God fearing husband. In March of 2004, God answered my prayers and blessed me with my husband, Roy.

Our family began to grow larger, when we adopted two new additions to the family and had a daughter together in 2007. I became the "Mother Hen". I'm the grandmother of five: three granddaughters, one biological and twin girls who are in my care today, and one grandson . We have a family of fourteen. My mother's wisdom came from Alice Dixson (my Mom). She was my best friend and she is missed dearly. I thank her for all the wisdom and advice that made me the mother, wife and a friend to many. I am the reflection of her mothering style. Her legacy lives on through me. I later met young mothers, in passing, that were in need of help. It seemed like I never meet *strangers*, because when I meet them I feel that God chose me to meet them. They would open up to me with all their troubles and discuss all their problems. I just wasn't able to help them the way I wanted, at that time.

I had to get creative real soon and I discussed a vision with my husband to open a nonprofit organization for homeless mothers. I shared with him my desire to buy property and fixing them up to house homeless mothers that were crying out for help to keep mothers and children safe. My husband agreed and said he thought it was a good idea. I then began to think, What should I name the organization?.... I thought the name: *Charismata* (means a Gift from God) would be a good name.

Charismata Homes opened it's doors in 2009. Charismata Homes has four locations: Westland, Farmington and Detroit. Charismata homes are transitional housing for homeless single mothers facing crises with their children. While in our program , the mothers receive supportive guidance, housing, education, food, clothing and community referrals. We identify the steps to achieve a stable, safe, and secure home for mothers and children. To learn more about our organization, please visit our website below: www.charismatahomesandcompany.com

Mariah Dixson The Stylist

IS SHOWING THE WORLD THAT SHE HAS MULTIPLE SKILLS. A DOUBLE THREAT IN THE BEAUTY INDUSTRY, A HAIR AND NAIL STYLIST.

by Carol Dorsey

Mariah was born February 20, 1994 and raised in Detroit Michigan. She graduated from Farmington High School. Mariah continued her education at Paul Mitchell the School Michigan in Sterling Heights, MI. Mariah understood from an early age that hair wasn't just an accessory, but that great hair is the key to feeling beautiful. Mariah specializes in nails, precision cutting and coloring, styling, and extensions with her artistic vision. She's always investing in her education in the beauty industry to master her many crafts and talents. She keeps up with the latest styles, techniques and trends as they appear on the fashion scene. It's her personal goal to continue to grow and excel in her craft and ultimately share all that she learns. Mariah continues to improve her skills through

international training and classes. Mariah is constantly evolving in the beauty industry by learning in hope of inspiring others. Her mission is to teach workshops, become a network educator, and a traveling stylist. Mariah's goal is to travel around the world

Serving as a stylist to not only women, but men as well. In addition, Mariah is also a dedicated nail technician. She likes to think that being blesses with endowment of her many skills, are compliments of her personality. When you find yourself in Mariah's hands, you're promised an enjoyable, professional as well as unforgettable experience.

Mariah's goal is to travel around the world serving as a stylist to not only women, but men as well.

Contact Mariah at:
Phone: (248) 497-6194

Website and 2016 Calendar Coming Soon!!!

COMING SOON!!!
MARIAH DIXSON

NEW SALON & 2016 CALENDAR

A full service salon with plenty of options to choose from!!!

IF YOU WANT TO LOOK YOUR BEST...VISIT THE BEST

COLORS OR STYLE THAT YOU'VE ALWAYS WANTED.

Martez Dixson (born 7/28/88), Music name Tez Rippa is an american Rapper from Detroit, Michigan. Tez is also an entrepreneur and a fireman from Detroit MI. He was born and raised in Detroit. Martez took his music serious in 2006. A talented artist as himself always knew he had skills to write 16 bars to a beat. Once he had saw how his music releases so much stress off his mind, he started to write more to clear his mind from everyday situations. Martez main goal is to take his music to a higher level. He also want to be a top artist in the industry and become an inspiration to our younger men. It's has been 8 years in the making and as a single father Martez has finally reach a point where he's comfortably discovered his purpose. While holding down a job as a fireman, Martez is going to push his music to the highest level Lord willing. Tez Rippa who is a part of RBBMG (RocBoi Music Group) is getting started and the main focus is to change his lifestyle. Martez is strongly driven and heavily determines to do so and his time is now! Also look out for his Clothing Line coming soon.

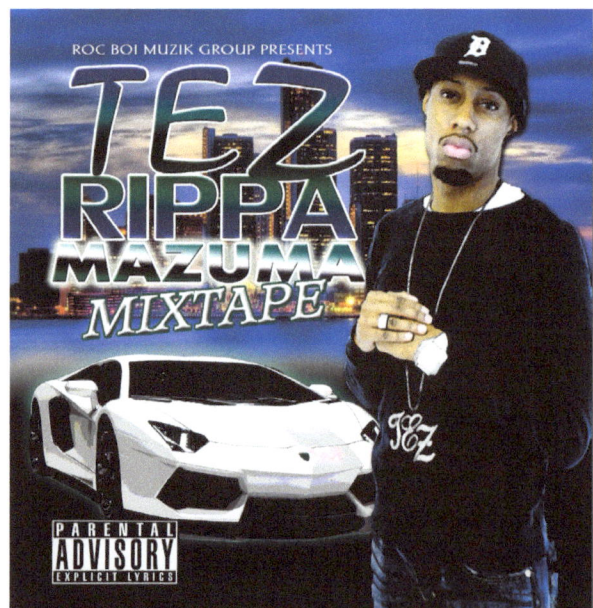

To download the Mixtape for FREE and for more information go to www.tezrippa.com.

Charismata Homes
PROGRAMS
ALL YEAR AROUND OUR PROGRAMS GIVE HOPE

One of the programs Charismata has been known for is the *Adopt a Family for Christmas Program*. During the second week of December, children and families receive gifts from generous members in our community.

We offer other progams, please visit our website if you would like to donate.

www.charismatahomesandcompany.com

Adopt-A-Family program has helped Metro Detroit families in need since 2013 and is coordinated by Charismata Homes organization and board members. The Adopt-A-Family program: Families in crisis, families struggling with illness, homelessness, domestic violence, poverty or unemployment.

During a typical year, the Adopt-A-Family program, with assistance from several individual and agencies, Charismata Homes organization in Detroit, Michigan has provided urgently needed assistance to over 20 disadvantaged families. Most of the beneficiaries are single parent households, children, and senior citizens. Our goal is to adopt 50 families or more by December 2016. Please help us reach our goal by donating toys, socks, hats, scarf's, gloves and personal kits. For more information, please contact us at us at 248-773-2866 or by email charismata630@gmail.com. Contact person Michelle Henry or staff members. Thank you in advance...

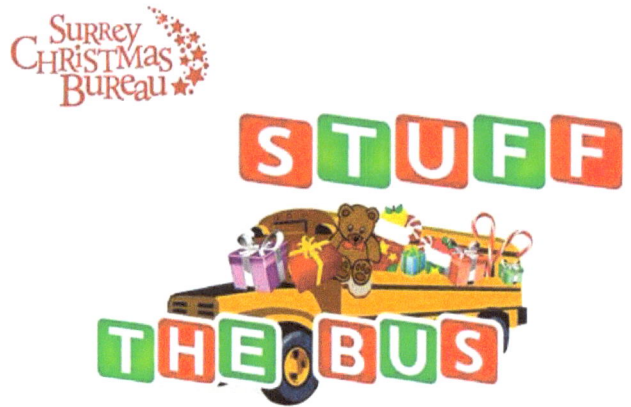

Sisters in Spirit Book Club
Adopt Families for Christmas.

A One-Stop Production Shop

MY TOUCH WEDDINGS OFFERS A PERSONAL TOUCH TO INSURE THE HIGHEST QUALITY PHOTOGRAPHS AND VIDEOS FOR EVERY CLIENT.

by Michelle Henry

Welcome to My Touch Weddings, owned and operated by DeOndre and Kyra Head! DeOndre, a Video Producer and Editor, experienced in various forms of production and performance and his wife, Kyra, a Photographer, shared a vision. Shortly after they were married in 2009, they decided, together they could make their vision a reality. This couple combined their talents and diligently worked together to create the "ULTIMATE" Production Company. This husband and wife duo were interested in designing a "One Stop Shop" which offers photography, videography, music production and a wide variety of other specialties.

DeOndre and Kyra offer their personal touch to insure that they capture the highest quality photographs and videos for every client. They work with each client to meet their individual needs, which allows their clients to feel comfortable entrusting reproduction of their special occasions to My Touch Weddings. They specialize in satisfying clients with the exceptional quality photography, videography and music production services that they provide.

My Touch Weddings is best known for photography and videography and state of the art photo booth services for special family events which include but, are not limited to; weddings, graduation parties, baby showers, engagement, maturity, and fashion photo shoots.

My Touch Weddings has been able to build their clientele by providing custom, professional services that encourage returning customers and recommendations. My Touch Weddings has a reputation based upon professional services that produces work in a timely manner, quality work based upon experience and dedication to excellence, courtesy, honesty, returning calls promptly and personally, flexible schedule and the ability to offer their customers ideas and advice that enhance their final product.

DeOndre' Head

Kyra Head

For advertisement
please call (248) 773-2866
or visit www.CHARISMATAhomesandcompany.com

www.ingramcontent.com/pod-product-compliance
Lightning Source LLC
Chambersburg PA
CBHW080253200326
41520CB00022B/7132